THIS BOOK BELONGS TO:

CONTACT INFORMATION	
NAME:	
ADDRESS:	
PHONE:	

START / END DATES

/ / TO / /

DEDICATION

This Firearms Record Book is dedicated to all the gun owner enthusiasts out there who want to record their gun collection and document their findings in the process.

You are my inspiration for producing books and I'm honored to be a part of keeping all of your Firearms Record Book notes and records organized.

This journal notebook will help you record the details of gun collection.

Thoughtfully put together with these sections to record: Master Index, Insurance Details, Gun Information, Acquisition & Disposition Information.

HOW TO USE THIS BOOK

The purpose of this book is to keep all of your Firearms notes all in one place. It will help keep you organized.

This Firearms Record Book will allow you to accurately document details about your gun collection.

Here are examples of the prompts for you to fill in and write about your experience in this book:

1. Master Index - Log the Gun, Serial Number, & Page Number.

2. Insurance Details - Write Company, Policy Number, Start/ End Date, Price, Coverage Type, Contact Info, & Notes.

3. Gun Information - Record Brand, Model, Action, Gauge or Caliber, Barrel, Sights, Stocks or Grips, Serial #, Condition, Unique Marks, Acquisition Date, Cost, Appraised Value, Where Acquired, Comments, History, Repairs, Sold To, & Selling Price.

4. Acquisition Information - Log Purchased From, Address, Contact Number, Date, Price Paid, ID Number, DOB, Condition, and Comments.

5. Disposition Information - Write Transfer/ Sold To, Address, Contact Number, Date, Price Paid, ID Number, DOB, Condition, Lost/ Stolen, Details, Notes for any other important information.

MASTER INDEX

GUN	SERIAL NUMBER	PAGE

| GUN | SERIAL NUMBER | PAGE |

MASTER INDEX

GUN	SERIAL NUMBER	PAGE
GUN	SERIAL NUMBER	PAGE

MASTER INDEX

GUN	SERIAL NUMBER	PAGE
GUN	SERIAL NUMBER	PAGE

MASTER INDEX

GUN	SERIAL NUMBER	PAGE
GUN	SERIAL NUMBER	PAGE

INSURANCE DETAILS

COMPANY	
POLICY NUMBER	
START DATE	END DATE
PRICE	
COVERAGE TYPE	
CONTACT NUMBER	
EMAIL	
FAX	
WEBSITE	
NOTES	

COMPANY	
POLICY NUMBER	
START DATE	END DATE
PRICE	
COVERAGE TYPE	
CONTACT NUMBER	
EMAIL	
FAX	
WEBSITE	
NOTES	

COMPANY	
POLICY NUMBER	
START DATE	END DATE
PRICE	
COVERAGE TYPE	
CONTACT NUMBER	
EMAIL	
FAX	
WEBSITE	
NOTES	

INSURANCE DETAILS

COMPANY	
POLICY NUMBER	
START DATE	END DATE
PRICE	
COVERAGE TYPE	
CONTACT NUMBER	
EMAIL	
FAX	
WEBSITE	
NOTES	

COMPANY	
POLICY NUMBER	
START DATE	END DATE
PRICE	
COVERAGE TYPE	
CONTACT NUMBER	
EMAIL	
FAX	
WEBSITE	
NOTES	

COMPANY	
POLICY NUMBER	
START DATE	END DATE
PRICE	
COVERAGE TYPE	
CONTACT NUMBER	
EMAIL	
FAX	
WEBSITE	
NOTES	

INSURANCE DETAILS

COMPANY	
POLICY NUMBER	
START DATE	END DATE
PRICE	
COVERAGE TYPE	
CONTACT NUMBER	
EMAIL	
FAX	
WEBSITE	
NOTES	

COMPANY	
POLICY NUMBER	
START DATE	END DATE
PRICE	
COVERAGE TYPE	
CONTACT NUMBER	
EMAIL	
FAX	
WEBSITE	
NOTES	

COMPANY	
POLICY NUMBER	
START DATE	END DATE
PRICE	
COVERAGE TYPE	
CONTACT NUMBER	
EMAIL	
FAX	
WEBSITE	
NOTES	

INSURANCE DETAILS

COMPANY	
POLICY NUMBER	
START DATE	END DATE
PRICE	
COVERAGE TYPE	
CONTACT NUMBER	
EMAIL	
FAX	
WEBSITE	
NOTES	

COMPANY	
POLICY NUMBER	
START DATE	END DATE
PRICE	
COVERAGE TYPE	
CONTACT NUMBER	
EMAIL	
FAX	
WEBSITE	
NOTES	

COMPANY	
POLICY NUMBER	
START DATE	END DATE
PRICE	
COVERAGE TYPE	
CONTACT NUMBER	
EMAIL	
FAX	
WEBSITE	
NOTES	

INSURANCE DETAILS

COMPANY	
POLICY NUMBER	
START DATE	END DATE
PRICE	
COVERAGE TYPE	
CONTACT NUMBER	
EMAIL	
FAX	
WEBSITE	
NOTES	

COMPANY	
POLICY NUMBER	
START DATE	END DATE
PRICE	
COVERAGE TYPE	
CONTACT NUMBER	
EMAIL	
FAX	
WEBSITE	
NOTES	

COMPANY	
POLICY NUMBER	
START DATE	END DATE
PRICE	
COVERAGE TYPE	
CONTACT NUMBER	
EMAIL	
FAX	
WEBSITE	
NOTES	

INSURANCE DETAILS

COMPANY	
POLICY NUMBER	
START DATE	END DATE
PRICE	
COVERAGE TYPE	
CONTACT NUMBER	
EMAIL	
FAX	
WEBSITE	
NOTES	

COMPANY	
POLICY NUMBER	
START DATE	END DATE
PRICE	
COVERAGE TYPE	
CONTACT NUMBER	
EMAIL	
FAX	
WEBSITE	
NOTES	

COMPANY	
POLICY NUMBER	
START DATE	END DATE
PRICE	
COVERAGE TYPE	
CONTACT NUMBER	
EMAIL	
FAX	
WEBSITE	
NOTES	

INSURANCE DETAILS

COMPANY	
POLICY NUMBER	
START DATE	END DATE
PRICE	
COVERAGE TYPE	
CONTACT NUMBER	
EMAIL	
FAX	
WEBSITE	
NOTES	

COMPANY	
POLICY NUMBER	
START DATE	END DATE
PRICE	
COVERAGE TYPE	
CONTACT NUMBER	
EMAIL	
FAX	
WEBSITE	
NOTES	

COMPANY	
POLICY NUMBER	
START DATE	END DATE
PRICE	
COVERAGE TYPE	
CONTACT NUMBER	
EMAIL	
FAX	
WEBSITE	
NOTES	

INSURANCE DETAILS

COMPANY	
POLICY NUMBER	
START DATE	END DATE
PRICE	
COVERAGE TYPE	
CONTACT NUMBER	
EMAIL	
FAX	
WEBSITE	
NOTES	

COMPANY	
POLICY NUMBER	
START DATE	END DATE
PRICE	
COVERAGE TYPE	
CONTACT NUMBER	
EMAIL	
FAX	
WEBSITE	
NOTES	

COMPANY	
POLICY NUMBER	
START DATE	END DATE
PRICE	
COVERAGE TYPE	
CONTACT NUMBER	
EMAIL	
FAX	
WEBSITE	
NOTES	

INSURANCE DETAILS

COMPANY	
POLICY NUMBER	
START DATE	END DATE
PRICE	
COVERAGE TYPE	
CONTACT NUMBER	
EMAIL	
FAX	
WEBSITE	
NOTES	

COMPANY	
POLICY NUMBER	
START DATE	END DATE
PRICE	
COVERAGE TYPE	
CONTACT NUMBER	
EMAIL	
FAX	
WEBSITE	
NOTES	

COMPANY	
POLICY NUMBER	
START DATE	END DATE
PRICE	
COVERAGE TYPE	
CONTACT NUMBER	
EMAIL	
FAX	
WEBSITE	
NOTES	

INSURANCE DETAILS

COMPANY	
POLICY NUMBER	
START DATE	END DATE
PRICE	
COVERAGE TYPE	
CONTACT NUMBER	
EMAIL	
FAX	
WEBSITE	
NOTES	

COMPANY	
POLICY NUMBER	
START DATE	END DATE
PRICE	
COVERAGE TYPE	
CONTACT NUMBER	
EMAIL	
FAX	
WEBSITE	
NOTES	

COMPANY	
POLICY NUMBER	
START DATE	END DATE
PRICE	
COVERAGE TYPE	
CONTACT NUMBER	
EMAIL	
FAX	
WEBSITE	
NOTES	

INSURANCE DETAILS

COMPANY	
POLICY NUMBER	
START DATE	END DATE
PRICE	
COVERAGE TYPE	
CONTACT NUMBER	
EMAIL	
FAX	
WEBSITE	
NOTES	

COMPANY	
POLICY NUMBER	
START DATE	END DATE
PRICE	
COVERAGE TYPE	
CONTACT NUMBER	
EMAIL	
FAX	
WEBSITE	
NOTES	

COMPANY	
POLICY NUMBER	
START DATE	END DATE
PRICE	
COVERAGE TYPE	
CONTACT NUMBER	
EMAIL	
FAX	
WEBSITE	
NOTES	

INSURANCE DETAILS

COMPANY	
POLICY NUMBER	
START DATE	END DATE
PRICE	
COVERAGE TYPE	
CONTACT NUMBER	
EMAIL	
FAX	
WEBSITE	
NOTES	

COMPANY	
POLICY NUMBER	
START DATE	END DATE
PRICE	
COVERAGE TYPE	
CONTACT NUMBER	
EMAIL	
FAX	
WEBSITE	
NOTES	

COMPANY	
POLICY NUMBER	
START DATE	END DATE
PRICE	
COVERAGE TYPE	
CONTACT NUMBER	
EMAIL	
FAX	
WEBSITE	
NOTES	

INSURANCE DETAILS

COMPANY	
POLICY NUMBER	
START DATE	END DATE
PRICE	
COVERAGE TYPE	
CONTACT NUMBER	
EMAIL	
FAX	
WEBSITE	
NOTES	

COMPANY	
POLICY NUMBER	
START DATE	END DATE
PRICE	
COVERAGE TYPE	
CONTACT NUMBER	
EMAIL	
FAX	
WEBSITE	
NOTES	

COMPANY	
POLICY NUMBER	
START DATE	END DATE
PRICE	
COVERAGE TYPE	
CONTACT NUMBER	
EMAIL	
FAX	
WEBSITE	
NOTES	

INSURANCE DETAILS

COMPANY	
POLICY NUMBER	
START DATE	END DATE
PRICE	
COVERAGE TYPE	
CONTACT NUMBER	
EMAIL	
FAX	
WEBSITE	
NOTES	

COMPANY	
POLICY NUMBER	
START DATE	END DATE
PRICE	
COVERAGE TYPE	
CONTACT NUMBER	
EMAIL	
FAX	
WEBSITE	
NOTES	

COMPANY	
POLICY NUMBER	
START DATE	END DATE
PRICE	
COVERAGE TYPE	
CONTACT NUMBER	
EMAIL	
FAX	
WEBSITE	
NOTES	

INSURANCE DETAILS

COMPANY	
POLICY NUMBER	
START DATE	END DATE
PRICE	
COVERAGE TYPE	
CONTACT NUMBER	
EMAIL	
FAX	
WEBSITE	
NOTES	

COMPANY	
POLICY NUMBER	
START DATE	END DATE
PRICE	
COVERAGE TYPE	
CONTACT NUMBER	
EMAIL	
FAX	
WEBSITE	
NOTES	

COMPANY	
POLICY NUMBER	
START DATE	END DATE
PRICE	
COVERAGE TYPE	
CONTACT NUMBER	
EMAIL	
FAX	
WEBSITE	
NOTES	

INSURANCE DETAILS

COMPANY	
POLICY NUMBER	
START DATE	END DATE
PRICE	
COVERAGE TYPE	
CONTACT NUMBER	
EMAIL	
FAX	
WEBSITE	
NOTES	

COMPANY	
POLICY NUMBER	
START DATE	END DATE
PRICE	
COVERAGE TYPE	
CONTACT NUMBER	
EMAIL	
FAX	
WEBSITE	
NOTES	

COMPANY	
POLICY NUMBER	
START DATE	END DATE
PRICE	
COVERAGE TYPE	
CONTACT NUMBER	
EMAIL	
FAX	
WEBSITE	
NOTES	

INSURANCE DETAILS

COMPANY	
POLICY NUMBER	
START DATE	END DATE
PRICE	
COVERAGE TYPE	
CONTACT NUMBER	
EMAIL	
FAX	
WEBSITE	
NOTES	

COMPANY	
POLICY NUMBER	
START DATE	END DATE
PRICE	
COVERAGE TYPE	
CONTACT NUMBER	
EMAIL	
FAX	
WEBSITE	
NOTES	

COMPANY	
POLICY NUMBER	
START DATE	END DATE
PRICE	
COVERAGE TYPE	
CONTACT NUMBER	
EMAIL	
FAX	
WEBSITE	
NOTES	

INSURANCE DETAILS

COMPANY	
POLICY NUMBER	
START DATE	END DATE
PRICE	
COVERAGE TYPE	
CONTACT NUMBER	
EMAIL	
FAX	
WEBSITE	
NOTES	

COMPANY	
POLICY NUMBER	
START DATE	END DATE
PRICE	
COVERAGE TYPE	
CONTACT NUMBER	
EMAIL	
FAX	
WEBSITE	
NOTES	

COMPANY	
POLICY NUMBER	
START DATE	END DATE
PRICE	
COVERAGE TYPE	
CONTACT NUMBER	
EMAIL	
FAX	
WEBSITE	
NOTES	

INSURANCE DETAILS

COMPANY	
POLICY NUMBER	
START DATE / END DATE	
PRICE	
COVERAGE TYPE	
CONTACT NUMBER	
EMAIL	
FAX	
WEBSITE	
NOTES	

COMPANY	
POLICY NUMBER	
START DATE / END DATE	
PRICE	
COVERAGE TYPE	
CONTACT NUMBER	
EMAIL	
FAX	
WEBSITE	
NOTES	

COMPANY	
POLICY NUMBER	
START DATE / END DATE	
PRICE	
COVERAGE TYPE	
CONTACT NUMBER	
EMAIL	
FAX	
WEBSITE	
NOTES	

INSURANCE DETAILS

COMPANY	
POLICY NUMBER	
START DATE	END DATE
PRICE	
COVERAGE TYPE	
CONTACT NUMBER	
EMAIL	
FAX	
WEBSITE	
NOTES	

COMPANY	
POLICY NUMBER	
START DATE	END DATE
PRICE	
COVERAGE TYPE	
CONTACT NUMBER	
EMAIL	
FAX	
WEBSITE	
NOTES	

COMPANY	
POLICY NUMBER	
START DATE	END DATE
PRICE	
COVERAGE TYPE	
CONTACT NUMBER	
EMAIL	
FAX	
WEBSITE	
NOTES	

INSURANCE DETAILS

COMPANY	
POLICY NUMBER	
START DATE	END DATE
PRICE	
COVERAGE TYPE	
CONTACT NUMBER	
EMAIL	
FAX	
WEBSITE	
NOTES	

COMPANY	
POLICY NUMBER	
START DATE	END DATE
PRICE	
COVERAGE TYPE	
CONTACT NUMBER	
EMAIL	
FAX	
WEBSITE	
NOTES	

COMPANY	
POLICY NUMBER	
START DATE	END DATE
PRICE	
COVERAGE TYPE	
CONTACT NUMBER	
EMAIL	
FAX	
WEBSITE	
NOTES	

INSURANCE DETAILS

COMPANY	
POLICY NUMBER	
START DATE / END DATE	
PRICE	
COVERAGE TYPE	
CONTACT NUMBER	
EMAIL	
FAX	
WEBSITE	
NOTES	

COMPANY	
POLICY NUMBER	
START DATE / END DATE	
PRICE	
COVERAGE TYPE	
CONTACT NUMBER	
EMAIL	
FAX	
WEBSITE	
NOTES	

COMPANY	
POLICY NUMBER	
START DATE / END DATE	
PRICE	
COVERAGE TYPE	
CONTACT NUMBER	
EMAIL	
FAX	
WEBSITE	
NOTES	

INSURANCE DETAILS

COMPANY	
POLICY NUMBER	
START DATE	END DATE
PRICE	
COVERAGE TYPE	
CONTACT NUMBER	
EMAIL	
FAX	
WEBSITE	
NOTES	

COMPANY	
POLICY NUMBER	
START DATE	END DATE
PRICE	
COVERAGE TYPE	
CONTACT NUMBER	
EMAIL	
FAX	
WEBSITE	
NOTES	

COMPANY	
POLICY NUMBER	
START DATE	END DATE
PRICE	
COVERAGE TYPE	
CONTACT NUMBER	
EMAIL	
FAX	
WEBSITE	
NOTES	

INSURANCE DETAILS

COMPANY	
POLICY NUMBER	
START DATE	END DATE
PRICE	
COVERAGE TYPE	
CONTACT NUMBER	
EMAIL	
FAX	
WEBSITE	
NOTES	

COMPANY	
POLICY NUMBER	
START DATE	END DATE
PRICE	
COVERAGE TYPE	
CONTACT NUMBER	
EMAIL	
FAX	
WEBSITE	
NOTES	

COMPANY	
POLICY NUMBER	
START DATE	END DATE
PRICE	
COVERAGE TYPE	
CONTACT NUMBER	
EMAIL	
FAX	
WEBSITE	
NOTES	

INSURANCE DETAILS

COMPANY	
POLICY NUMBER	
START DATE	END DATE
PRICE	
COVERAGE TYPE	
CONTACT NUMBER	
EMAIL	
FAX	
WEBSITE	
NOTES	

COMPANY	
POLICY NUMBER	
START DATE	END DATE
PRICE	
COVERAGE TYPE	
CONTACT NUMBER	
EMAIL	
FAX	
WEBSITE	
NOTES	

COMPANY	
POLICY NUMBER	
START DATE	END DATE
PRICE	
COVERAGE TYPE	
CONTACT NUMBER	
EMAIL	
FAX	
WEBSITE	
NOTES	

INSURANCE DETAILS

COMPANY	
POLICY NUMBER	
START DATE	END DATE
PRICE	
COVERAGE TYPE	
CONTACT NUMBER	
EMAIL	
FAX	
WEBSITE	
NOTES	

COMPANY	
POLICY NUMBER	
START DATE	END DATE
PRICE	
COVERAGE TYPE	
CONTACT NUMBER	
EMAIL	
FAX	
WEBSITE	
NOTES	

COMPANY	
POLICY NUMBER	
START DATE	END DATE
PRICE	
COVERAGE TYPE	
CONTACT NUMBER	
EMAIL	
FAX	
WEBSITE	
NOTES	

INSURANCE DETAILS

COMPANY	
POLICY NUMBER	
START DATE	END DATE
PRICE	
COVERAGE TYPE	
CONTACT NUMBER	
EMAIL	
FAX	
WEBSITE	
NOTES	

COMPANY	
POLICY NUMBER	
START DATE	END DATE
PRICE	
COVERAGE TYPE	
CONTACT NUMBER	
EMAIL	
FAX	
WEBSITE	
NOTES	

COMPANY	
POLICY NUMBER	
START DATE	END DATE
PRICE	
COVERAGE TYPE	
CONTACT NUMBER	
EMAIL	
FAX	
WEBSITE	
NOTES	

INSURANCE DETAILS

COMPANY	
POLICY NUMBER	
START DATE	END DATE
PRICE	
COVERAGE TYPE	
CONTACT NUMBER	
EMAIL	
FAX	
WEBSITE	
NOTES	

COMPANY	
POLICY NUMBER	
START DATE	END DATE
PRICE	
COVERAGE TYPE	
CONTACT NUMBER	
EMAIL	
FAX	
WEBSITE	
NOTES	

COMPANY	
POLICY NUMBER	
START DATE	END DATE
PRICE	
COVERAGE TYPE	
CONTACT NUMBER	
EMAIL	
FAX	
WEBSITE	
NOTES	

INFORMATION

BRAND		MODEL	
ACTION		GAUGE OR CALIBER	
BARREL		SIGHTS	
STOCKS OR GRIPS			
SERIAL #		CONDITION	
UNIQUE MARKS			
ACQUISITION DATE		COST		APPRAISED VALUE	
WHERE ACQUIRED			
COMMENTS			
HISTORY			

REPAIRS	DATE	COST

SOLD TO	
DATE	SELLING PRICE

INFORMATION

BRAND		MODEL	
ACTION		GAUGE OR CALIBER	
BARREL		SIGHTS	
STOCKS OR GRIPS			
SERIAL #		CONDITION	
UNIQUE MARKS			
ACQUISITION DATE		COST	APPRAISED VALUE
WHERE ACQUIRED			
COMMENTS			
HISTORY			

REPAIRS	DATE	COST

SOLD TO	
DATE	SELLING PRICE

INFORMATION

BRAND		MODEL			
ACTION		GAUGE OR CALIBER			
BARREL		SIGHTS			
STOCKS OR GRIPS					
SERIAL #		CONDITION			
UNIQUE MARKS					
ACQUISITION DATE		COST		APPRAISED VALUE	
WHERE ACQUIRED					
COMMENTS					
HISTORY					

REPAIRS	DATE	COST

SOLD TO	
DATE	SELLING PRICE

INFORMATION

BRAND		MODEL		
ACTION		GAUGE OR CALIBER		
BARREL		SIGHTS		
STOCKS OR GRIPS				
SERIAL #		CONDITION		
UNIQUE MARKS				
ACQUISITION DATE		COST		APPRAISED VALUE	
WHERE ACQUIRED				
COMMENTS				
HISTORY				

REPAIRS	DATE	COST

SOLD TO	
DATE	
SELLING PRICE	

INFORMATION

40

BRAND		MODEL	
ACTION		GAUGE OR CALIBER	
BARREL		SIGHTS	
STOCKS OR GRIPS			
SERIAL #		CONDITION	
UNIQUE MARKS			
ACQUISITION DATE		COST	APPRAISED VALUE
WHERE ACQUIRED			
COMMENTS			
HISTORY			

REPAIRS	DATE	COST

SOLD TO	
DATE	SELLING PRICE

INFORMATION

BRAND		MODEL		
ACTION		GAUGE OR CALIBER		
BARREL		SIGHTS		
STOCKS OR GRIPS				
SERIAL #		CONDITION		
UNIQUE MARKS				
ACQUISITION DATE		COST		APPRAISED VALUE
WHERE ACQUIRED				
COMMENTS				
HISTORY				

REPAIRS	DATE	COST

SOLD TO	
DATE	SELLING PRICE

INFORMATION

BRAND		MODEL			
ACTION		GAUGE OR CALIBER			
BARREL		SIGHTS			
STOCKS OR GRIPS					
SERIAL #		CONDITION			
UNIQUE MARKS					
ACQUISITION DATE		COST		APPRAISED VALUE	
WHERE ACQUIRED					
COMMENTS					
HISTORY					

REPAIRS	DATE	COST

SOLD TO			
DATE		SELLING PRICE	

INFORMATION

BRAND		MODEL	
ACTION		GAUGE OR CALIBER	
BARREL		SIGHTS	
STOCKS OR GRIPS			
SERIAL #		CONDITION	
UNIQUE MARKS			
ACQUISITION DATE		COST	APPRAISED VALUE
WHERE ACQUIRED			
COMMENTS			
HISTORY			

REPAIRS	DATE	COST

SOLD TO	
DATE	SELLING PRICE

INFORMATION

BRAND		MODEL	
ACTION		GAUGE OR CALIBER	
BARREL		SIGHTS	
STOCKS OR GRIPS			
SERIAL #		CONDITION	
UNIQUE MARKS			

ACQUISITION DATE		COST		APPRAISED VALUE	
WHERE ACQUIRED					
COMMENTS					
HISTORY					

REPAIRS	DATE	COST

SOLD TO			
DATE		SELLING PRICE	

INFORMATION

BRAND		MODEL		
ACTION		GAUGE OR CALIBER		
BARREL		SIGHTS		
STOCKS OR GRIPS				
SERIAL #		CONDITION		
UNIQUE MARKS				
ACQUISITION DATE		COST		APPRAISED VALUE	
WHERE ACQUIRED				
COMMENTS				
HISTORY				

REPAIRS	DATE	COST

SOLD TO			
DATE		SELLING PRICE	

INFORMATION

BRAND		MODEL			
ACTION		GAUGE OR CALIBER			
BARREL		SIGHTS			
STOCKS OR GRIPS					
SERIAL #		CONDITION			
UNIQUE MARKS					
ACQUISITION DATE		COST		APPRAISED VALUE	
WHERE ACQUIRED					
COMMENTS					
HISTORY					

REPAIRS	DATE	COST

SOLD TO	
DATE	SELLING PRICE

INFORMATION

BRAND		MODEL	
ACTION		GAUGE OR CALIBER	
BARREL		SIGHTS	
STOCKS OR GRIPS			
SERIAL #		CONDITION	
UNIQUE MARKS			
ACQUISITION DATE		COST		APPRAISED VALUE	
WHERE ACQUIRED			
COMMENTS			
HISTORY			

REPAIRS	DATE	COST

SOLD TO	
DATE		SELLING PRICE	

INFORMATION

BRAND		MODEL		
ACTION		GAUGE OR CALIBER		
BARREL		SIGHTS		
STOCKS OR GRIPS				
SERIAL #		CONDITION		
UNIQUE MARKS				
ACQUISITION DATE		COST		APPRAISED VALUE	
WHERE ACQUIRED				
COMMENTS				
HISTORY				

REPAIRS	DATE	COST

SOLD TO	
DATE	SELLING PRICE

INFORMATION

BRAND		MODEL			
ACTION		GAUGE OR CALIBER			
BARREL		SIGHTS			
STOCKS OR GRIPS					
SERIAL #		CONDITION			
UNIQUE MARKS					
ACQUISITION DATE		COST		APPRAISED VALUE	
WHERE ACQUIRED					
COMMENTS					
HISTORY					

REPAIRS	DATE	COST

SOLD TO			
DATE		SELLING PRICE	

INFORMATION

BRAND		MODEL			
ACTION		GAUGE OR CALIBER			
BARREL		SIGHTS			
STOCKS OR GRIPS					
SERIAL #		CONDITION			
UNIQUE MARKS					
ACQUISITION DATE		COST		APPRAISED VALUE	
WHERE ACQUIRED					
COMMENTS					
HISTORY					

REPAIRS	DATE	COST

SOLD TO			
DATE		SELLING PRICE	

INFORMATION

BRAND		MODEL	
ACTION		GAUGE OR CALIBER	
BARREL		SIGHTS	
STOCKS OR GRIPS			
SERIAL #		CONDITION	
UNIQUE MARKS			
ACQUISITION DATE		COST		APPRAISED VALUE	
WHERE ACQUIRED			
COMMENTS			
HISTORY			

REPAIRS	DATE	COST

SOLD TO	
DATE		SELLING PRICE	

INFORMATION

BRAND		MODEL	
ACTION		GAUGE OR CALIBER	
BARREL		SIGHTS	
STOCKS OR GRIPS			
SERIAL #		CONDITION	
UNIQUE MARKS			
ACQUISITION DATE		COST		APPRAISED VALUE	
WHERE ACQUIRED			
COMMENTS			
HISTORY			

REPAIRS	DATE	COST

SOLD TO	
DATE	SELLING PRICE

INFORMATION

BRAND		MODEL		
ACTION		GAUGE OR CALIBER		
BARREL		SIGHTS		
STOCKS OR GRIPS				
SERIAL #		CONDITION		
UNIQUE MARKS				
ACQUISITION DATE		COST		APPRAISED VALUE	
WHERE ACQUIRED				
COMMENTS				
HISTORY				

REPAIRS	DATE	COST

SOLD TO			
DATE		SELLING PRICE	

INFORMATION

BRAND		MODEL		
ACTION		GAUGE OR CALIBER		
BARREL		SIGHTS		
STOCKS OR GRIPS				
SERIAL #		CONDITION		
UNIQUE MARKS				
ACQUISITION DATE		COST		APPRAISED VALUE
WHERE ACQUIRED				
COMMENTS				
HISTORY				

REPAIRS	DATE	COST

SOLD TO			
DATE		SELLING PRICE	

INFORMATION

BRAND		MODEL	
ACTION		GAUGE OR CALIBER	
BARREL		SIGHTS	
STOCKS OR GRIPS			
SERIAL #		CONDITION	
UNIQUE MARKS			
ACQUISITION DATE		COST	APPRAISED VALUE
WHERE ACQUIRED			
COMMENTS			
HISTORY			

REPAIRS	DATE	COST

SOLD TO	
DATE	SELLING PRICE

INFORMATION

BRAND		MODEL		
ACTION		GAUGE OR CALIBER		
BARREL		SIGHTS		
STOCKS OR GRIPS				
SERIAL #		CONDITION		
UNIQUE MARKS				
ACQUISITION DATE		COST		APPRAISED VALUE
WHERE ACQUIRED				
COMMENTS				
HISTORY				

REPAIRS	DATE	COST

SOLD TO	
DATE	SELLING PRICE

INFORMATION

BRAND		MODEL	
ACTION		GAUGE OR CALIBER	
BARREL		SIGHTS	
STOCKS OR GRIPS			
SERIAL #		CONDITION	
UNIQUE MARKS			
ACQUISITION DATE		COST	APPRAISED VALUE
WHERE ACQUIRED			
COMMENTS			
HISTORY			

REPAIRS	DATE	COST

SOLD TO			
DATE		SELLING PRICE	

INFORMATION

BRAND		MODEL			
ACTION		GAUGE OR CALIBER			
BARREL		SIGHTS			
STOCKS OR GRIPS					
SERIAL #		CONDITION			
UNIQUE MARKS					
ACQUISITION DATE		COST		APPRAISED VALUE	
WHERE ACQUIRED					
COMMENTS					
HISTORY					

REPAIRS	DATE	COST

SOLD TO			
DATE		SELLING PRICE	

INFORMATION

BRAND		MODEL		
ACTION		GAUGE OR CALIBER		
BARREL		SIGHTS		
STOCKS OR GRIPS				
SERIAL #		CONDITION		
UNIQUE MARKS				
ACQUISITION DATE		COST		APPRAISED VALUE	
WHERE ACQUIRED				
COMMENTS				
HISTORY				

REPAIRS	DATE	COST

SOLD TO	
DATE	SELLING PRICE

INFORMATION

BRAND		MODEL			
ACTION		GAUGE OR CALIBER			
BARREL		SIGHTS			
STOCKS OR GRIPS					
SERIAL #		CONDITION			
UNIQUE MARKS					
ACQUISITION DATE		COST		APPRAISED VALUE	
WHERE ACQUIRED					
COMMENTS					
HISTORY					

REPAIRS	DATE	COST

SOLD TO	
DATE	SELLING PRICE

INFORMATION

BRAND		MODEL		
ACTION		GAUGE OR CALIBER		
BARREL		SIGHTS		
STOCKS OR GRIPS				
SERIAL #		CONDITION		
UNIQUE MARKS				
ACQUISITION DATE		COST		APPRAISED VALUE	
WHERE ACQUIRED				
COMMENTS				
HISTORY				

REPAIRS	DATE	COST

SOLD TO			
DATE		SELLING PRICE	

INFORMATION

BRAND		MODEL			
ACTION		GAUGE OR CALIBER			
BARREL		SIGHTS			
STOCKS OR GRIPS					
SERIAL #		CONDITION			
UNIQUE MARKS					
ACQUISITION DATE		COST		APPRAISED VALUE	
WHERE ACQUIRED					
COMMENTS					
HISTORY					

REPAIRS	DATE	COST

SOLD TO	
DATE	SELLING PRICE

INFORMATION

BRAND		MODEL	
ACTION		GAUGE OR CALIBER	
BARREL		SIGHTS	
STOCKS OR GRIPS			
SERIAL #		CONDITION	
UNIQUE MARKS			
ACQUISITION DATE		COST	APPRAISED VALUE
WHERE ACQUIRED			
COMMENTS			
HISTORY			

REPAIRS	DATE	COST

SOLD TO			
DATE		SELLING PRICE	

INFORMATION

BRAND		MODEL			
ACTION		GAUGE OR CALIBER			
BARREL		SIGHTS			
STOCKS OR GRIPS					
SERIAL #		CONDITION			
UNIQUE MARKS					
ACQUISITION DATE		COST		APPRAISED VALUE	
WHERE ACQUIRED					
COMMENTS					
HISTORY					

REPAIRS	DATE	COST

SOLD TO			
DATE		SELLING PRICE	

INFORMATION

BRAND		MODEL			
ACTION		GAUGE OR CALIBER			
BARREL		SIGHTS			
STOCKS OR GRIPS					
SERIAL #		CONDITION			
UNIQUE MARKS					
ACQUISITION DATE		COST		APPRAISED VALUE	
WHERE ACQUIRED					
COMMENTS					
HISTORY					

REPAIRS	DATE	COST

SOLD TO			
DATE		SELLING PRICE	

INFORMATION

BRAND		MODEL		
ACTION		GAUGE OR CALIBER		
BARREL		SIGHTS		
STOCKS OR GRIPS				
SERIAL #		CONDITION		
UNIQUE MARKS				
ACQUISITION DATE		COST		APPRAISED VALUE	
WHERE ACQUIRED				
COMMENTS				
HISTORY				

REPAIRS	DATE	COST

SOLD TO	
DATE	SELLING PRICE

INFORMATION

BRAND		MODEL	
ACTION		GAUGE OR CALIBER	
BARREL		SIGHTS	
STOCKS OR GRIPS			
SERIAL #		CONDITION	
UNIQUE MARKS			
ACQUISITION DATE		COST	APPRAISED VALUE
WHERE ACQUIRED			
COMMENTS			
HISTORY			

REPAIRS	DATE	COST

SOLD TO			
DATE		SELLING PRICE	

INFORMATION

BRAND		MODEL			
ACTION		GAUGE OR CALIBER			
BARREL		SIGHTS			
STOCKS OR GRIPS					
SERIAL #		CONDITION			
UNIQUE MARKS					
ACQUISITION DATE		COST		APPRAISED VALUE	
WHERE ACQUIRED					
COMMENTS					
HISTORY					

REPAIRS	DATE	COST

SOLD TO	
DATE	SELLING PRICE

INFORMATION

BRAND		MODEL		
ACTION		GAUGE OR CALIBER		
BARREL		SIGHTS		
STOCKS OR GRIPS				
SERIAL #		CONDITION		
UNIQUE MARKS				
ACQUISITION DATE		COST		APPRAISED VALUE
WHERE ACQUIRED				
COMMENTS				
HISTORY				

REPAIRS	DATE	COST

SOLD TO			
DATE		SELLING PRICE	

INFORMATION

BRAND		MODEL			
ACTION		GAUGE OR CALIBER			
BARREL		SIGHTS			
STOCKS OR GRIPS					
SERIAL #		CONDITION			
UNIQUE MARKS					
ACQUISITION DATE		COST		APPRAISED VALUE	
WHERE ACQUIRED					
COMMENTS					
HISTORY					

REPAIRS	DATE	COST

SOLD TO			
DATE		SELLING PRICE	

INFORMATION

BRAND		MODEL	
ACTION		GAUGE OR CALIBER	
BARREL		SIGHTS	
STOCKS OR GRIPS			
SERIAL #		CONDITION	
UNIQUE MARKS			
ACQUISITION DATE		COST	APPRAISED VALUE
WHERE ACQUIRED			
COMMENTS			
HISTORY			

REPAIRS	DATE	COST

SOLD TO	
DATE	SELLING PRICE

INFORMATION

BRAND		MODEL			
ACTION		GAUGE OR CALIBER			
BARREL		SIGHTS			
STOCKS OR GRIPS					
SERIAL #		CONDITION			
UNIQUE MARKS					
ACQUISITION DATE		COST		APPRAISED VALUE	
WHERE ACQUIRED					
COMMENTS					
HISTORY					

REPAIRS	DATE	COST

SOLD TO	
DATE	SELLING PRICE

INFORMATION

BRAND		MODEL		
ACTION		GAUGE OR CALIBER		
BARREL		SIGHTS		
STOCKS OR GRIPS				
SERIAL #		CONDITION		
UNIQUE MARKS				
ACQUISITION DATE		COST		APPRAISED VALUE	
WHERE ACQUIRED				
COMMENTS				
HISTORY				

REPAIRS	DATE	COST

SOLD TO			
DATE		SELLING PRICE	

INFORMATION

BRAND		MODEL		
ACTION		GAUGE OR CALIBER		
BARREL		SIGHTS		
STOCKS OR GRIPS				
SERIAL #		CONDITION		
UNIQUE MARKS				
ACQUISITION DATE		COST		APPRAISED VALUE	
WHERE ACQUIRED				
COMMENTS				
HISTORY				

REPAIRS	DATE	COST

SOLD TO	
DATE	SELLING PRICE

INFORMATION

BRAND		MODEL		
ACTION		GAUGE OR CALIBER		
BARREL		SIGHTS		
STOCKS OR GRIPS				
SERIAL #		CONDITION		
UNIQUE MARKS				
ACQUISITION DATE		COST		APPRAISED VALUE
WHERE ACQUIRED				
COMMENTS				
HISTORY				

REPAIRS	DATE	COST

SOLD TO	
DATE	SELLING PRICE

INFORMATION

BRAND		MODEL		
ACTION		GAUGE OR CALIBER		
BARREL		SIGHTS		
STOCKS OR GRIPS				
SERIAL #		CONDITION		
UNIQUE MARKS				
ACQUISITION DATE		COST		APPRAISED VALUE
WHERE ACQUIRED				
COMMENTS				
HISTORY				

REPAIRS	DATE	COST

SOLD TO	
DATE	SELLING PRICE

INFORMATION

BRAND		MODEL	
ACTION		GAUGE OR CALIBER	
BARREL		SIGHTS	
STOCKS OR GRIPS			
SERIAL #		CONDITION	
UNIQUE MARKS			
ACQUISITION DATE		COST	APPRAISED VALUE
WHERE ACQUIRED			
COMMENTS			
HISTORY			

REPAIRS	DATE	COST

SOLD TO			
DATE		SELLING PRICE	

INFORMATION

BRAND		MODEL			
ACTION		GAUGE OR CALIBER			
BARREL		SIGHTS			
STOCKS OR GRIPS					
SERIAL #		CONDITION			
UNIQUE MARKS					
ACQUISITION DATE		COST		APPRAISED VALUE	
WHERE ACQUIRED					
COMMENTS					
HISTORY					

REPAIRS	DATE	COST

SOLD TO			
DATE		SELLING PRICE	

INFORMATION

BRAND		MODEL	
ACTION		GAUGE OR CALIBER	
BARREL		SIGHTS	
STOCKS OR GRIPS			
SERIAL #		CONDITION	
UNIQUE MARKS			
ACQUISITION DATE		COST		APPRAISED VALUE	
WHERE ACQUIRED			
COMMENTS			
HISTORY			

REPAIRS	DATE	COST

SOLD TO			
DATE		SELLING PRICE	

INFORMATION

BRAND		MODEL			
ACTION		GAUGE OR CALIBER			
BARREL		SIGHTS			
STOCKS OR GRIPS					
SERIAL #		CONDITION			
UNIQUE MARKS					
ACQUISITION DATE		COST		APPRAISED VALUE	
WHERE ACQUIRED					
COMMENTS					
HISTORY					

REPAIRS	DATE	COST

SOLD TO	
DATE	SELLING PRICE

INFORMATION

BRAND		MODEL		
ACTION		GAUGE OR CALIBER		
BARREL		SIGHTS		
STOCKS OR GRIPS				
SERIAL #		CONDITION		
UNIQUE MARKS				
ACQUISITION DATE		COST		APPRAISED VALUE	
WHERE ACQUIRED				
COMMENTS				
HISTORY				

REPAIRS	DATE	COST

SOLD TO	
DATE	SELLING PRICE

INFORMATION

BRAND		MODEL			
ACTION		GAUGE OR CALIBER			
BARREL		SIGHTS			
STOCKS OR GRIPS					
SERIAL #		CONDITION			
UNIQUE MARKS					
ACQUISITION DATE		COST		APPRAISED VALUE	
WHERE ACQUIRED					
COMMENTS					
HISTORY					

REPAIRS	DATE	COST

SOLD TO			
DATE		SELLING PRICE	

INFORMATION

BRAND		MODEL		
ACTION		GAUGE OR CALIBER		
BARREL		SIGHTS		
STOCKS OR GRIPS				
SERIAL #		CONDITION		
UNIQUE MARKS				
ACQUISITION DATE		COST		APPRAISED VALUE
WHERE ACQUIRED				
COMMENTS				
HISTORY				

REPAIRS	DATE	COST

SOLD TO	
DATE	SELLING PRICE

INFORMATION

BRAND		MODEL			
ACTION		GAUGE OR CALIBER			
BARREL		SIGHTS			
STOCKS OR GRIPS					
SERIAL #		CONDITION			
UNIQUE MARKS					
ACQUISITION DATE		COST		APPRAISED VALUE	
WHERE ACQUIRED					
COMMENTS					
HISTORY					

REPAIRS	DATE	COST

SOLD TO			
DATE		SELLING PRICE	

INFORMATION

BRAND		MODEL		
ACTION		GAUGE OR CALIBER		
BARREL		SIGHTS		
STOCKS OR GRIPS				
SERIAL #		CONDITION		
UNIQUE MARKS				
ACQUISITION DATE		COST		APPRAISED VALUE
WHERE ACQUIRED				
COMMENTS				
HISTORY				

REPAIRS	DATE	COST

SOLD TO	
DATE	SELLING PRICE

INFORMATION

BRAND		MODEL	
ACTION		GAUGE OR CALIBER	
BARREL		SIGHTS	
STOCKS OR GRIPS			
SERIAL #		CONDITION	
UNIQUE MARKS			
ACQUISITION DATE		COST	APPRAISED VALUE
WHERE ACQUIRED			
COMMENTS			
HISTORY			

REPAIRS	DATE	COST

SOLD TO	
DATE	SELLING PRICE

INFORMATION

BRAND		MODEL	
ACTION		GAUGE OR CALIBER	
BARREL		SIGHTS	
STOCKS OR GRIPS			
SERIAL #		CONDITION	
UNIQUE MARKS			
ACQUISITION DATE		COST		APPRAISED VALUE	
WHERE ACQUIRED			
COMMENTS			
HISTORY			

REPAIRS	DATE	COST

SOLD TO	
DATE	SELLING PRICE

INFORMATION

BRAND		MODEL			
ACTION		GAUGE OR CALIBER			
BARREL		SIGHTS			
STOCKS OR GRIPS					
SERIAL #		CONDITION			
UNIQUE MARKS					
ACQUISITION DATE		COST		APPRAISED VALUE	
WHERE ACQUIRED					
COMMENTS					
HISTORY					

REPAIRS	DATE	COST

SOLD TO			
DATE		SELLING PRICE	

INFORMATION

BRAND		MODEL		
ACTION		GAUGE OR CALIBER		
BARREL		SIGHTS		
STOCKS OR GRIPS				
SERIAL #		CONDITION		
UNIQUE MARKS				
ACQUISITION DATE		COST		APPRAISED VALUE
WHERE ACQUIRED				
COMMENTS				
HISTORY				

REPAIRS	DATE	COST

SOLD TO	
DATE	SELLING PRICE

INFORMATION

BRAND		MODEL			
ACTION		GAUGE OR CALIBER			
BARREL		SIGHTS			
STOCKS OR GRIPS					
SERIAL #		CONDITION			
UNIQUE MARKS					
ACQUISITION DATE		COST		APPRAISED VALUE	
WHERE ACQUIRED					
COMMENTS					
HISTORY					

REPAIRS	DATE	COST

SOLD TO	
DATE	SELLING PRICE

INFORMATION

BRAND		MODEL	
ACTION		GAUGE OR CALIBER	
BARREL		SIGHTS	
STOCKS OR GRIPS			
SERIAL #		CONDITION	
UNIQUE MARKS			
ACQUISITION DATE		COST		APPRAISED VALUE	
WHERE ACQUIRED			
COMMENTS			
HISTORY			

REPAIRS	DATE	COST

SOLD TO	
DATE	SELLING PRICE

ACQUISITION INFORMATION

PURCHASED FROM	
ADDRESS	
CONTACT NUMBER	
DATE	PRICE PAID
ID NUMBER	D.O.B.
CONDITION	
COMMENTS	

DISPOSITION INFORMATION

TRANSFER / SOLD TO	
ADDRESS	
CONTACT NUMBER	
DATE	PRICE PAID
ID NUMBER	D.O.B.
LOST / STOLEN	CONDITION
DETAILS	

IN THE EVENT OF MY DEMISE I WANT THIS FIREARM TO GO TO	

NOTES

ACQUISITION INFORMATION

PURCHASED FROM	
ADDRESS	
CONTACT NUMBER	

DATE		PRICE PAID	
ID NUMBER		D.O.B.	

CONDITION	
COMMENTS	

DISPOSITION INFORMATION

TRANSFER / SOLD TO	
ADDRESS	
CONTACT NUMBER	

DATE		PRICE PAID	
ID NUMBER		D.O.B.	
LOST / STOLEN		CONDITION	

DETAILS	
IN THE EVENT OF MY DEMISE I WANT THIS FIREARM TO GO TO	

NOTES

ACQUISITION INFORMATION

PURCHASED FROM	
ADDRESS	
CONTACT NUMBER	
DATE	PRICE PAID
ID NUMBER	D.O.B.
CONDITION	
COMMENTS	

DISPOSITION INFORMATION

TRANSFER / SOLD TO	
ADDRESS	
CONTACT NUMBER	
DATE	PRICE PAID
ID NUMBER	D.O.B.
LOST / STOLEN	CONDITION
DETAILS	

IN THE EVENT OF MY DEMISE I WANT THIS FIREARM TO GO TO	

NOTES

ACQUISITION INFORMATION

PURCHASED FROM	
ADDRESS	
CONTACT NUMBER	
DATE	PRICE PAID
ID NUMBER	D.O.B.
CONDITION	
COMMENTS	

DISPOSITION INFORMATION

TRANSFER / SOLD TO	
ADDRESS	
CONTACT NUMBER	
DATE	PRICE PAID
ID NUMBER	D.O.B.
LOST / STOLEN	CONDITION
DETAILS	

IN THE EVENT OF MY DEMISE I WANT THIS FIREARM TO GO TO	

NOTES

ACQUISITION INFORMATION

PURCHASED FROM	
ADDRESS	
CONTACT NUMBER	
DATE	PRICE PAID
ID NUMBER	D.O.B.
CONDITION	
COMMENTS	

DISPOSITION INFORMATION

TRANSFER / SOLD TO	
ADDRESS	
CONTACT NUMBER	
DATE	PRICE PAID
ID NUMBER	D.O.B.
LOST / STOLEN	CONDITION
DETAILS	

IN THE EVENT OF MY DEMISE I WANT THIS FIREARM TO GO TO	

NOTES

ACQUISITION INFORMATION

PURCHASED FROM	
ADDRESS	
CONTACT NUMBER	
DATE	PRICE PAID
ID NUMBER	D.O.B.
CONDITION	
COMMENTS	

DISPOSITION INFORMATION

TRANSFER / SOLD TO	
ADDRESS	
CONTACT NUMBER	
DATE	PRICE PAID
ID NUMBER	D.O.B.
LOST / STOLEN	CONDITION
DETAILS	

IN THE EVENT OF MY DEMISE I WANT THIS FIREARM TO GO TO	

NOTES

ACQUISITION INFORMATION

PURCHASED FROM	
ADDRESS	
CONTACT NUMBER	
DATE	PRICE PAID
ID NUMBER	D.O.B.
CONDITION	
COMMENTS	

DISPOSITION INFORMATION

TRANSFER / SOLD TO	
ADDRESS	
CONTACT NUMBER	
DATE	PRICE PAID
ID NUMBER	D.O.B.
LOST / STOLEN	CONDITION
DETAILS	

IN THE EVENT OF MY DEMISE I WANT THIS FIREARM TO GO TO	

NOTES

ACQUISITION INFORMATION

PURCHASED FROM	
ADDRESS	
CONTACT NUMBER	
DATE	PRICE PAID
ID NUMBER	D.O.B.
CONDITION	
COMMENTS	

DISPOSITION INFORMATION

TRANSFER / SOLD TO	
ADDRESS	
CONTACT NUMBER	
DATE	PRICE PAID
ID NUMBER	D.O.B.
LOST / STOLEN	CONDITION
DETAILS	

IN THE EVENT OF MY DEMISE I WANT THIS FIREARM TO GO TO	

NOTES

ACQUISITION INFORMATION

PURCHASED FROM	
ADDRESS	
CONTACT NUMBER	
DATE	PRICE PAID
ID NUMBER	D.O.B.
CONDITION	
COMMENTS	

DISPOSITION INFORMATION

TRANSFER / SOLD TO	
ADDRESS	
CONTACT NUMBER	
DATE	PRICE PAID
ID NUMBER	D.O.B.
LOST / STOLEN	CONDITION
DETAILS	

IN THE EVENT OF MY DEMISE I WANT THIS FIREARM TO GO TO	

NOTES

ACQUISITION INFORMATION

PURCHASED FROM	
ADDRESS	
CONTACT NUMBER	
DATE	PRICE PAID
ID NUMBER	D.O.B.
CONDITION	
COMMENTS	

DISPOSITION INFORMATION

TRANSFER / SOLD TO	
ADDRESS	
CONTACT NUMBER	
DATE	PRICE PAID
ID NUMBER	D.O.B.
LOST / STOLEN	CONDITION
DETAILS	

IN THE EVENT OF MY DEMISE I WANT THIS FIREARM TO GO TO	

NOTES

ACQUISITION INFORMATION

PURCHASED FROM	
ADDRESS	
CONTACT NUMBER	
DATE	PRICE PAID
ID NUMBER	D.O.B.
CONDITION	
COMMENTS	

DISPOSITION INFORMATION

TRANSFER / SOLD TO	
ADDRESS	
CONTACT NUMBER	
DATE	PRICE PAID
ID NUMBER	D.O.B.
LOST / STOLEN	CONDITION
DETAILS	

IN THE EVENT OF MY DEMISE I WANT THIS FIREARM TO GO TO	

NOTES

ACQUISITION INFORMATION

PURCHASED FROM	
ADDRESS	
CONTACT NUMBER	
DATE	PRICE PAID
ID NUMBER	D.O.B.
CONDITION	
COMMENTS	

DISPOSITION INFORMATION

TRANSFER / SOLD TO	
ADDRESS	
CONTACT NUMBER	
DATE	PRICE PAID
ID NUMBER	D.O.B.
LOST / STOLEN	CONDITION
DETAILS	

IN THE EVENT OF MY DEMISE I WANT THIS FIREARM TO GO TO	

NOTES

ACQUISITION INFORMATION

PURCHASED FROM	
ADDRESS	
CONTACT NUMBER	
DATE	PRICE PAID
ID NUMBER	D.O.B.
CONDITION	
COMMENTS	

DISPOSITION INFORMATION

TRANSFER / SOLD TO	
ADDRESS	
CONTACT NUMBER	
DATE	PRICE PAID
ID NUMBER	D.O.B
LOST / STOLEN	CONDITION
DETAILS	

IN THE EVENT OF MY DEMISE I WANT THIS FIREARM TO GO TO	

NOTES

ACQUISITION INFORMATION

PURCHASED FROM	
ADDRESS	
CONTACT NUMBER	

DATE		PRICE PAID	
ID NUMBER		D.O.B.	

CONDITION	
COMMENTS	

DISPOSITION INFORMATION

TRANSFER / SOLD TO	
ADDRESS	
CONTACT NUMBER	

DATE		PRICE PAID	
ID NUMBER		D.O.B.	
LOST / STOLEN		CONDITION	

DETAILS	
IN THE EVENT OF MY DEMISE I WANT THIS FIREARM TO GO TO	

NOTES

ACQUISITION INFORMATION

PURCHASED FROM	
ADDRESS	
CONTACT NUMBER	
DATE	PRICE PAID
ID NUMBER	D.O.B.
CONDITION	
COMMENTS	

DISPOSITION INFORMATION

TRANSFER / SOLD TO	
ADDRESS	
CONTACT NUMBER	
DATE	PRICE PAID
ID NUMBER	D.O.B.
LOST / STOLEN	CONDITION
DETAILS	

IN THE EVENT OF MY DEMISE I WANT THIS FIREARM TO GO TO	

NOTES

ACQUISITION INFORMATION

PURCHASED FROM	
ADDRESS	
CONTACT NUMBER	
DATE		PRICE PAID	
ID NUMBER		D.O.B.	
CONDITION	
COMMENTS	

DISPOSITION INFORMATION

TRANSFER / SOLD TO	
ADDRESS	
CONTACT NUMBER	
DATE		PRICE PAID	
ID NUMBER		D.O.B.	
LOST / STOLEN		CONDITION	
DETAILS	

IN THE EVENT OF MY DEMISE I WANT THIS FIREARM TO GO TO	

NOTES

ACQUISITION INFORMATION

PURCHASED FROM	
ADDRESS	
CONTACT NUMBER	
DATE	PRICE PAID
ID NUMBER	D.O.B.
CONDITION	
COMMENTS	

DISPOSITION INFORMATION

TRANSFER / SOLD TO	
ADDRESS	
CONTACT NUMBER	
DATE	PRICE PAID
ID NUMBER	D.O.B.
LOST / STOLEN	CONDITION
DETAILS	

IN THE EVENT OF MY DEMISE I WANT THIS FIREARM TO GO TO	

NOTES

ACQUISITION INFORMATION

PURCHASED FROM	
ADDRESS	
CONTACT NUMBER	
DATE	PRICE PAID
ID NUMBER	D.O.B.
CONDITION	
COMMENTS	

DISPOSITION INFORMATION

TRANSFER / SOLD TO	
ADDRESS	
CONTACT NUMBER	
DATE	PRICE PAID
ID NUMBER	D.O.B.
LOST / STOLEN	CONDITION
DETAILS	

IN THE EVENT OF MY DEMISE I WANT THIS FIREARM TO GO TO	

NOTES

ACQUISITION INFORMATION

PURCHASED FROM	
ADDRESS	
CONTACT NUMBER	
DATE	PRICE PAID
ID NUMBER	D.O.B.
CONDITION	
COMMENTS	

DISPOSITION INFORMATION

TRANSFER / SOLD TO	
ADDRESS	
CONTACT NUMBER	
DATE	PRICE PAID
ID NUMBER	D.O.B.
LOST / STOLEN	CONDITION
DETAILS	

IN THE EVENT OF MY DEMISE I WANT THIS FIREARM TO GO TO	

NOTES

ACQUISITION INFORMATION

PURCHASED FROM	
ADDRESS	
CONTACT NUMBER	

DATE		PRICE PAID	
ID NUMBER		D.O.B.	

CONDITION	
COMMENTS	

DISPOSITION INFORMATION

TRANSFER / SOLD TO	
ADDRESS	
CONTACT NUMBER	

DATE		PRICE PAID	
ID NUMBER		D.O.B.	
LOST / STOLEN		CONDITION	

DETAILS	

IN THE EVENT OF MY DEMISE I WANT THIS FIREARM TO GO TO	

NOTES

ACQUISITION INFORMATION

PURCHASED FROM	
ADDRESS	
CONTACT NUMBER	
DATE	PRICE PAID
ID NUMBER	D.O.B.
CONDITION	
COMMENTS	

DISPOSITION INFORMATION

TRANSFER / SOLD TO	
ADDRESS	
CONTACT NUMBER	
DATE	PRICE PAID
ID NUMBER	D.O.B.
LOST / STOLEN	CONDITION
DETAILS	

IN THE EVENT OF MY DEMISE I WANT THIS FIREARM TO GO TO	

NOTES

ACQUISITION INFORMATION

PURCHASED FROM	
ADDRESS	
CONTACT NUMBER	

DATE		PRICE PAID	
ID NUMBER		D.O.B.	

CONDITION	
COMMENTS	

DISPOSITION INFORMATION

TRANSFER / SOLD TO	
ADDRESS	
CONTACT NUMBER	

DATE		PRICE PAID	
ID NUMBER		D.O.B.	
LOST / STOLEN		CONDITION	

DETAILS	

IN THE EVENT OF MY DEMISE I WANT THIS FIREARM TO GO TO	

NOTES

ACQUISITION INFORMATION

PURCHASED FROM	
ADDRESS	
CONTACT NUMBER	
DATE	PRICE PAID
ID NUMBER	D.O.B.
CONDITION	
COMMENTS	

DISPOSITION INFORMATION

TRANSFER / SOLD TO	
ADDRESS	
CONTACT NUMBER	
DATE	PRICE PAID
ID NUMBER	D.O.B.
LOST / STOLEN	CONDITION
DETAILS	

IN THE EVENT OF MY DEMISE I WANT THIS FIREARM TO GO TO	

NOTES

ACQUISITION INFORMATION

PURCHASED FROM	
ADDRESS	
CONTACT NUMBER	
DATE	PRICE PAID
ID NUMBER	D.O.B.
CONDITION	
COMMENTS	

DISPOSITION INFORMATION

TRANSFER / SOLD TO	
ADDRESS	
CONTACT NUMBER	
DATE	PRICE PAID
ID NUMBER	D.O.B.
LOST / STOLEN	CONDITION
DETAILS	

IN THE EVENT OF MY DEMISE I WANT THIS FIREARM TO GO TO	

NOTES

ACQUISITION INFORMATION

PURCHASED FROM	
ADDRESS	
CONTACT NUMBER	
DATE	PRICE PAID
ID NUMBER	D.O.B.
CONDITION	
COMMENTS	

DISPOSITION INFORMATION

TRANSFER / SOLD TO	
ADDRESS	
CONTACT NUMBER	
DATE	PRICE PAID
ID NUMBER	D.O.B.
LOST / STOLEN	CONDITION
DETAILS	

IN THE EVENT OF MY DEMISE I WANT THIS FIREARM TO GO TO	

NOTES

ACQUISITION INFORMATION

PURCHASED FROM	
ADDRESS	
CONTACT NUMBER	
DATE	PRICE PAID
ID NUMBER	D.O.B.
CONDITION	
COMMENTS	

DISPOSITION INFORMATION

TRANSFER / SOLD TO	
ADDRESS	
CONTACT NUMBER	
DATE	PRICE PAID
ID NUMBER	D.O.B.
LOST / STOLEN	CONDITION
DETAILS	

IN THE EVENT OF MY DEMISE I WANT THIS FIREARM TO GO TO	

NOTES

ACQUISITION INFORMATION

PURCHASED FROM	
ADDRESS	
CONTACT NUMBER	

DATE		PRICE PAID	
ID NUMBER		D.O.B.	

CONDITION	
COMMENTS	

DISPOSITION INFORMATION

TRANSFER / SOLD TO	
ADDRESS	
CONTACT NUMBER	

DATE		PRICE PAID	
ID NUMBER		D.O.B.	
LOST / STOLEN		CONDITION	

DETAILS	

IN THE EVENT OF MY DEMISE I WANT THIS FIREARM TO GO TO	

NOTES

ACQUISITION INFORMATION

PURCHASED FROM	
ADDRESS	
CONTACT NUMBER	
DATE	PRICE PAID
ID NUMBER	D.O.B.
CONDITION	
COMMENTS	

DISPOSITION INFORMATION

TRANSFER / SOLD TO	
ADDRESS	
CONTACT NUMBER	
DATE	PRICE PAID
ID NUMBER	D.O.B.
LOST / STOLEN	CONDITION
DETAILS	

IN THE EVENT OF MY DEMISE I WANT THIS FIREARM TO GO TO	

NOTES

ACQUISITION INFORMATION

PURCHASED FROM	
ADDRESS	
CONTACT NUMBER	
DATE	PRICE PAID
ID NUMBER	D.O.B.
CONDITION	
COMMENTS	

DISPOSITION INFORMATION

TRANSFER / SOLD TO	
ADDRESS	
CONTACT NUMBER	
DATE	PRICE PAID
ID NUMBER	D.O.B.
LOST / STOLEN	CONDITION
DETAILS	

IN THE EVENT OF MY DEMISE I WANT THIS FIREARM TO GO TO	

NOTES

ACQUISITION INFORMATION

PURCHASED FROM	
ADDRESS	
CONTACT NUMBER	
DATE	PRICE PAID
ID NUMBER	D.O.B.
CONDITION	
COMMENTS	

DISPOSITION INFORMATION

TRANSFER / SOLD TO	
ADDRESS	
CONTACT NUMBER	
DATE	PRICE PAID
ID NUMBER	D.O.B.
LOST / STOLEN	CONDITION
DETAILS	

IN THE EVENT OF MY DEMISE I WANT THIS FIREARM TO GO TO	

NOTES

ACQUISITION INFORMATION

PURCHASED FROM	
ADDRESS	
CONTACT NUMBER	
DATE	PRICE PAID
ID NUMBER	D.O.B.
CONDITION	
COMMENTS	

DISPOSITION INFORMATION

TRANSFER / SOLD TO	
ADDRESS	
CONTACT NUMBER	
DATE	PRICE PAID
ID NUMBER	D.O.B.
LOST / STOLEN	CONDITION
DETAILS	

IN THE EVENT OF MY DEMISE I WANT THIS FIREARM TO GO TO	

NOTES

ACQUISITION INFORMATION

PURCHASED FROM	
ADDRESS	
CONTACT NUMBER	
DATE		PRICE PAID	
ID NUMBER		D.O.B.	
CONDITION	
COMMENTS	

DISPOSITION INFORMATION

TRANSFER / SOLD TO	
ADDRESS	
CONTACT NUMBER	
DATE		PRICE PAID	
ID NUMBER		D.O.B	
LOST / STOLEN		CONDITION	
DETAILS	

IN THE EVENT OF MY DEMISE I WANT THIS FIREARM TO GO TO	

NOTES

ACQUISITION INFORMATION

PURCHASED FROM	
ADDRESS	
CONTACT NUMBER	
DATE	PRICE PAID
ID NUMBER	D.O.B.
CONDITION	
COMMENTS	

DISPOSITION INFORMATION

TRANSFER / SOLD TO	
ADDRESS	
CONTACT NUMBER	
DATE	PRICE PAID
ID NUMBER	D.O.B.
LOST / STOLEN	CONDITION
DETAILS	

IN THE EVENT OF MY DEMISE I WANT THIS FIREARM TO GO TO	

NOTES

ACQUISITION INFORMATION

PURCHASED FROM	
ADDRESS	
CONTACT NUMBER	
DATE	PRICE PAID
ID NUMBER	D.O.B.
CONDITION	
COMMENTS	

DISPOSITION INFORMATION

TRANSFER / SOLD TO	
ADDRESS	
CONTACT NUMBER	
DATE	PRICE PAID
ID NUMBER	D.O.B.
LOST / STOLEN	CONDITION
DETAILS	

IN THE EVENT OF MY DEMISE I WANT THIS FIREARM TO GO TO	

NOTES

ACQUISITION INFORMATION

PURCHASED FROM	
ADDRESS	
CONTACT NUMBER	
DATE	PRICE PAID
ID NUMBER	D.O.B.
CONDITION	
COMMENTS	

DISPOSITION INFORMATION

TRANSFER / SOLD TO	
ADDRESS	
CONTACT NUMBER	
DATE	PRICE PAID
ID NUMBER	D.O.B.
LOST / STOLEN	CONDITION
DETAILS	

IN THE EVENT OF MY DEMISE I WANT THIS FIREARM TO GO TO	

NOTES

ACQUISITION INFORMATION

PURCHASED FROM	
ADDRESS	
CONTACT NUMBER	

DATE		PRICE PAID	
ID NUMBER		D.O.B.	

CONDITION	
COMMENTS	

DISPOSITION INFORMATION

TRANSFER / SOLD TO	
ADDRESS	
CONTACT NUMBER	

DATE		PRICE PAID	
ID NUMBER		D.O.B.	
LOST / STOLEN		CONDITION	

DETAILS	

IN THE EVENT OF MY DEMISE I WANT THIS FIREARM TO GO TO	

NOTES

ACQUISITION INFORMATION

PURCHASED FROM	
ADDRESS	
CONTACT NUMBER	
DATE	PRICE PAID
ID NUMBER	D.O.B.
CONDITION	
COMMENTS	

DISPOSITION INFORMATION

TRANSFER / SOLD TO	
ADDRESS	
CONTACT NUMBER	
DATE	PRICE PAID
ID NUMBER	D.O.B.
LOST / STOLEN	CONDITION
DETAILS	

IN THE EVENT OF MY DEMISE I WANT THIS FIREARM TO GO TO	

NOTES

ACQUISITION INFORMATION

PURCHASED FROM	
ADDRESS	
CONTACT NUMBER	
DATE	PRICE PAID
ID NUMBER	D.O.B.
CONDITION	
COMMENTS	

DISPOSITION INFORMATION

TRANSFER / SOLD TO	
ADDRESS	
CONTACT NUMBER	
DATE	PRICE PAID
ID NUMBER	D.O.B.
LOST / STOLEN	CONDITION
DETAILS	

IN THE EVENT OF MY DEMISE I WANT THIS FIREARM TO GO TO	

NOTES

ACQUISITION INFORMATION

PURCHASED FROM	
ADDRESS	
CONTACT NUMBER	
DATE	PRICE PAID
ID NUMBER	D.O.B.
CONDITION	
COMMENTS	

DISPOSITION INFORMATION

TRANSFER / SOLD TO	
ADDRESS	
CONTACT NUMBER	
DATE	PRICE PAID
ID NUMBER	D.O.B.
LOST / STOLEN	CONDITION
DETAILS	

IN THE EVENT OF MY DEMISE I WANT THIS FIREARM TO GO TO	

NOTES

ACQUISITION INFORMATION

PURCHASED FROM	
ADDRESS	
CONTACT NUMBER	
DATE	PRICE PAID
ID NUMBER	D.O.B.
CONDITION	
COMMENTS	

DISPOSITION INFORMATION

TRANSFER / SOLD TO	
ADDRESS	
CONTACT NUMBER	
DATE	PRICE PAID
ID NUMBER	D.O.B.
LOST / STOLEN	CONDITION
DETAILS	

IN THE EVENT OF MY DEMISE I WANT THIS FIREARM TO GO TO	

NOTES

ACQUISITION INFORMATION

PURCHASED FROM	
ADDRESS	
CONTACT NUMBER	
DATE	PRICE PAID
ID NUMBER	D.O.B.
CONDITION	
COMMENTS	

DISPOSITION INFORMATION

TRANSFER / SOLD TO	
ADDRESS	
CONTACT NUMBER	
DATE	PRICE PAID
ID NUMBER	D.O.B.
LOST / STOLEN	CONDITION
DETAILS	

IN THE EVENT OF MY DEMISE I WANT THIS FIREARM TO GO TO	

NOTES

ACQUISITION INFORMATION

PURCHASED FROM	
ADDRESS	
CONTACT NUMBER	
DATE		PRICE PAID	
ID NUMBER		D.O.B.	
CONDITION	
COMMENTS	

DISPOSITION INFORMATION

TRANSFER / SOLD TO	
ADDRESS	
CONTACT NUMBER	
DATE		PRICE PAID	
ID NUMBER		D.O.B.	
LOST / STOLEN		CONDITION	
DETAILS	

IN THE EVENT OF MY DEMISE I WANT THIS FIREARM TO GO TO	

NOTES

ACQUISITION INFORMATION

PURCHASED FROM	
ADDRESS	
CONTACT NUMBER	

DATE		PRICE PAID	
ID NUMBER		D.O.B.	

CONDITION	
COMMENTS	

DISPOSITION INFORMATION

TRANSFER / SOLD TO	
ADDRESS	
CONTACT NUMBER	

DATE		PRICE PAID	
ID NUMBER		D.O.B.	
LOST / STOLEN		CONDITION	

DETAILS	

IN THE EVENT OF MY DEMISE I WANT THIS FIREARM TO GO TO	

NOTES

ACQUISITION INFORMATION

PURCHASED FROM	
ADDRESS	
CONTACT NUMBER	

DATE		PRICE PAID	
ID NUMBER		D.O.B.	

CONDITION	
COMMENTS	

DISPOSITION INFORMATION

TRANSFER / SOLD TO	
ADDRESS	
CONTACT NUMBER	

DATE		PRICE PAID	
ID NUMBER		D.O.B.	
LOST / STOLEN		CONDITION	

DETAILS	

IN THE EVENT OF MY DEMISE I WANT THIS FIREARM TO GO TO	

NOTES

ACQUISITION INFORMATION

PURCHASED FROM	
ADDRESS	
CONTACT NUMBER	
DATE	PRICE PAID
ID NUMBER	D.O.B.
CONDITION	
COMMENTS	

DISPOSITION INFORMATION

TRANSFER / SOLD TO	
ADDRESS	
CONTACT NUMBER	
DATE	PRICE PAID
ID NUMBER	D.O.B.
LOST / STOLEN	CONDITION
DETAILS	

IN THE EVENT OF MY DEMISE I WANT THIS FIREARM TO GO TO	

NOTES

ACQUISITION INFORMATION

PURCHASED FROM	
ADDRESS	
CONTACT NUMBER	
DATE	PRICE PAID
ID NUMBER	D.O.B.
CONDITION	
COMMENTS	

DISPOSITION INFORMATION

TRANSFER / SOLD TO	
ADDRESS	
CONTACT NUMBER	
DATE	PRICE PAID
ID NUMBER	D.O.B.
LOST / STOLEN	CONDITION
DETAILS	

IN THE EVENT OF MY DEMISE I WANT THIS FIREARM TO GO TO	

NOTES

ACQUISITION INFORMATION

PURCHASED FROM	
ADDRESS	
CONTACT NUMBER	

DATE		PRICE PAID	
ID NUMBER		D.O.B.	

CONDITION	
COMMENTS	

DISPOSITION INFORMATION

TRANSFER / SOLD TO	
ADDRESS	
CONTACT NUMBER	

DATE		PRICE PAID	
ID NUMBER		D.O.B.	
LOST / STOLEN		CONDITION	

DETAILS	

IN THE EVENT OF MY DEMISE I WANT THIS FIREARM TO GO TO	

NOTES

ACQUISITION INFORMATION

PURCHASED FROM	
ADDRESS	
CONTACT NUMBER	
DATE	PRICE PAID
ID NUMBER	D.O.B.
CONDITION	
COMMENTS	

DISPOSITION INFORMATION

TRANSFER / SOLD TO	
ADDRESS	
CONTACT NUMBER	
DATE	PRICE PAID
ID NUMBER	D.O.B.
LOST / STOLEN	CONDITION
DETAILS	

IN THE EVENT OF MY DEMISE I WANT THIS FIREARM TO GO TO	

NOTES

ACQUISITION INFORMATION

PURCHASED FROM	
ADDRESS	
CONTACT NUMBER	
DATE	PRICE PAID
ID NUMBER	D.O.B.
CONDITION	
COMMENTS	

DISPOSITION INFORMATION

TRANSFER / SOLD TO	
ADDRESS	
CONTACT NUMBER	
DATE	PRICE PAID
ID NUMBER	D.O.B.
LOST / STOLEN	CONDITION
DETAILS	

IN THE EVENT OF MY DEMISE I WANT THIS FIREARM TO GO TO	

NOTES

ACQUISITION INFORMATION

PURCHASED FROM	
ADDRESS	
CONTACT NUMBER	
DATE	PRICE PAID
ID NUMBER	D.O.B.
CONDITION	
COMMENTS	

DISPOSITION INFORMATION

TRANSFER / SOLD TO	
ADDRESS	
CONTACT NUMBER	
DATE	PRICE PAID
ID NUMBER	D.O.B.
LOST / STOLEN	CONDITION
DETAILS	

IN THE EVENT OF MY DEMISE I WANT THIS FIREARM TO GO TO	

NOTES

ACQUISITION INFORMATION

PURCHASED FROM	
ADDRESS	
CONTACT NUMBER	
DATE	PRICE PAID
ID NUMBER	D.O.B.
CONDITION	
COMMENTS	

DISPOSITION INFORMATION

TRANSFER / SOLD TO	
ADDRESS	
CONTACT NUMBER	
DATE	PRICE PAID
ID NUMBER	D.O.B.
LOST / STOLEN	CONDITION
DETAILS	

IN THE EVENT OF MY DEMISE I WANT THIS FIREARM TO GO TO	

NOTES

ACQUISITION INFORMATION

PURCHASED FROM	
ADDRESS	
CONTACT NUMBER	

DATE		PRICE PAID	
ID NUMBER		D.O.B.	

CONDITION	
COMMENTS	

DISPOSITION INFORMATION

TRANSFER / SOLD TO	
ADDRESS	
CONTACT NUMBER	

DATE		PRICE PAID	
ID NUMBER		D.O.B.	
LOST / STOLEN		CONDITION	

DETAILS	

IN THE EVENT OF MY DEMISE I WANT THIS FIREARM TO GO TO	

NOTES

ACQUISITION INFORMATION

PURCHASED FROM	
ADDRESS	
CONTACT NUMBER	
DATE	PRICE PAID
ID NUMBER	D.O.B.
CONDITION	
COMMENTS	

DISPOSITION INFORMATION

TRANSFER / SOLD TO	
ADDRESS	
CONTACT NUMBER	
DATE	PRICE PAID
ID NUMBER	D.O.B.
LOST / STOLEN	CONDITION
DETAILS	

IN THE EVENT OF MY DEMISE I WANT THIS FIREARM TO GO TO	

NOTES

ACQUISITION INFORMATION

PURCHASED FROM	
ADDRESS	
CONTACT NUMBER	
DATE	PRICE PAID
ID NUMBER	D.O.B.
CONDITION	
COMMENTS	

DISPOSITION INFORMATION

TRANSFER / SOLD TO	
ADDRESS	
CONTACT NUMBER	
DATE	PRICE PAID
ID NUMBER	D.O.B.
LOST / STOLEN	CONDITION
DETAILS	

IN THE EVENT OF MY DEMISE I WANT THIS FIREARM TO GO TO	

NOTES

ACQUISITION INFORMATION

PURCHASED FROM	
ADDRESS	
CONTACT NUMBER	

DATE		PRICE PAID	
ID NUMBER		D.O.B.	

CONDITION	
COMMENTS	

DISPOSITION INFORMATION

TRANSFER / SOLD TO	
ADDRESS	
CONTACT NUMBER	

DATE		PRICE PAID	
ID NUMBER		D.O.B.	
LOST / STOLEN		CONDITION	

DETAILS	

IN THE EVENT OF MY DEMISE I WANT THIS FIREARM TO GO TO	

NOTES

ACQUISITION INFORMATION

PURCHASED FROM	
ADDRESS	
CONTACT NUMBER	
DATE		PRICE PAID	
ID NUMBER		D.O.B.	
CONDITION	
COMMENTS	

DISPOSITION INFORMATION

TRANSFER / SOLD TO	
ADDRESS	
CONTACT NUMBER	
DATE		PRICE PAID	
ID NUMBER		D.O.B.	
LOST / STOLEN		CONDITION	
DETAILS	

IN THE EVENT OF MY DEMISE I WANT THIS FIREARM TO GO TO	

NOTES